THE RISEN CHRIST
AND THE ETHERIC CHRIST

BY THE SAME AUTHOR:

The Catacombs
Growing Point

Christian Community Press

THE RISEN CHRIST AND THE ETHERIC CHRIST

Two lectures given to the Anthroposophical Society of America in New York, April 22nd and 29th, 1949

by

ALFRED HEIDENREICH

Rudolf Steiner Press

Rudolf Steiner Press
Hillside House, The Square
Forest Row, RH18 5ES

www.rudolfsteinerpress.com

Published by Rudolf Steiner Press 2013

First published in 1969. Reprinted 2013

A catalogue record for this book is available from the British Library

ISBN 978 1 85584 391 2

Cover by Andrew Morgan Design
Printed and bound in Great Britain by 4edge Limited, Hockley

PUBLISHER'S NOTE

These lectures were given by Alfred Heidenreich to members of the Anthroposophical Society in America, not as public lectures. It must, therefore, be remembered that they assume a familiarity by his audience with the published lectures of Rudolf Steiner. On the one hand, therefore, they are an exposition of his work for those seeking a deeper understanding of it. On the other hand, they show Alfred Heidenreich's remarkable gift for illuminating the vital questions concerning the Being of Christ as it is shown in the writings of the New Testament through his understanding and imaginative presentation of the implications of some of Steiner's teaching. It is for this reason that, when Dr. Heidenreich offered these lectures shortly before his death, the present publishers gladly accepted them for publication to a wider audience. After twenty years, there are now many more people open to hear and even seeking such explanations as are here offered.

THE FALL FROM PARADISE AND ITS REDEMPTION BY CHRIST

Tonight we are undertaking a very serious task; historically, one not undertaken for some fifteen hundred years or more. Not since the first three Christian centuries have any thinking people presumed to speak in detail about those intimate, esoteric problems connected with the nature of the resurrection body of Christ. In order to trace historical dates we shall have to go back to the days when the Gnostics—that sect in early Christian times which considered such subjects—were an honoured part of early Christianity; to that time when such matters were still discussed by the seekers and also by the teachers of Christian thought and knowledge. In retrospect we can perhaps understand why the discussion of these deeply esoteric subjects had to be discontinued.

The suppression of the Gnostic movement in the fourth, fifth and sixth centuries, although it robbed Western civilization of a vast measure of spiritual truth, can possibly be justified because of the fact that they were almost one-sided in their emphasis on the spiritual, the cosmic nature of Christ. If the Gnostic movement had survived it seems possible in the light of history that knowledge of the cosmic nature of Christ might indeed have been handed down and survived. But there was great danger that the fact of the incarnation of the cosmic Christ in the historic Jesus would have been lost because it was the Gnostics who developed the theory of "the apparent body of Christ," a theory known as Docetism. This theory suggested that either someone else died on the cross (some had the idea that Simon of Cyrene took the place of Jesus in the last moment) or, as other Gnostics taught, Christ had really withdrawn from the body of Jesus before the Passion.

There was great danger that these thinkers, who had largely drawn their concepts from the ancient mysteries, might indeed have missed the vital fact of the full indwelling of Christ in Jesus throughout the hours on the cross, which ultimately produced the resurrection body. Because this fundamental truth that "the Word became flesh and dwelt among us" might have been lost, it becomes possible to see some justification for the fact that the Gnostics were suppressed and finally exterminated.

We should gather from this brief recapitulation that if now after fifteen hundred years or so we reconsider such a tremendous subject, we are indeed making history. Actually this gathering of Anthroposophists tonight could truthfully be described as a continuation of those earnest meetings of early church fathers in the second and third centuries where, in the inner circles of the instructed and partly initiated, these things were discussed. Nothing less fits the historic situation in which we find ourselves today. We can approach this subject only with great humility and with full appreciation of the fact that our knowledge and faculties, and our efforts in the study of Rudolf Steiner's writings, are not yet adequate to deal with it in a satisfactory manner.

I take my start from certain considerations contained in the cycle "Building Stones Towards an

Understanding of The Mystery of Golgotha". In one of those lectures Rudolf Steiner speaks about the nature of human death. He introduces this subject by pointing out that death in the animal world and death in the human sphere are two totally different phenomena, a fact which does not immediately appeal to popular understanding. So far as we can see there is great similarity between the two. But Steiner, viewing it more inwardly, says that from an adequate study of the physiology of the animal, every organ, the total process of the animal body, indicates that it is organized for death. In the actual formation, in the very substance, in the cooperative functioning of those organs which make up the animal body, there is implicit an indication of an organization towards death; that when its organs reach a certain stage of development they cease to function and die. Then the Group-soul withdraws from that particular part of its physical manifestation. But, he continues to say, if you study the organs of the human body in the same way you find no such indication; you find in fact that the human body is organized for immortality. Steiner says that the human Group-soul, the Species-soul which makes the human body a manifestation of the species MAN and produces this individual body as the bearer of an individual human spirit—this Group-soul should operate in such a way as to render the body immortal. It would not withdraw from its parts but would dwell in these bodies as long as the Earth exists. Then he points out the spiritual problem posed by the fact that obviously we die and leave behind a corpse, the manifestation of death. How then did this come to be? He says that one discovers that death or dying issues from the soul; that it is through the soul that the possibility and then the necessity for death occurs. This is what lies hidden in that old and mysterious expression "original sin", which is not anything that an individual commits but which refers to that event which we describe as "The Fall". As a moral event this has so affected human souls that they carry the necessity of death into the human body. Human death cannot be understood by any concept formed along the lines of natural scientific thought. It can be comprehended only if one understands that a moral event can have a natural result; that the moral order of existence can affect the natural order; that at a certain time, through the event described in the Old Testament as "The Fall," an impulse was given to the human soul which gradually so corrupted the organs of life in the human body that they received the necessity of death. Then through the great act of Christ *this impulse was undone.*

But between this act and ultimate redemption there lies a vast process and many detailed facts which we may now presume to consider. Where can we trace in Man spiritually, psychologically, medically, symptoms of this sickness originally produced by the soul, which has so transformed and corrupted human nature that it must die? I think we may point to four functions in man where a deep natural instinct would show some evidence. Our *sense perception* is the first process to consider. This has become crude, purely external, materially defined and circumscribed. We no longer see the aura, that spiritual counterpart of the material world, not even in living things. In this connection we may cite the book of Genesis: "Their eyes were opened and they saw that they were naked." The human figure itself is only a focal point for the fact that as a result of The Fall we see all things naked, that is to say in material outline only. Deep in the human soul is a sense which will always respond to the suggestion that there is something wrong with us as a species, though we may regard ourselves as natural and normal human beings, that in fact our sense perception is more material than it need be.

The second functional sphere in man is *breathing*, which we take more or less for granted, breathing out carbon dioxide and breathing in oxygen, which we use up so completely that were this room to be hermetically sealed and we to go on breathing, by tomorrow morning we should all be dead. Literally we breathe in the breath of life, and breathe out the breath of death. In Eastern tradition the fact is not simply taken for granted that the plant world, through the opposite process of assimilation, establishes an equilibrium. Rather it is felt that there is a kind of moral compensation; the plants in their innocence redeem the guilt of man which shows itself in his poisonous breath. This moral view of nature makes an Eastern mind deeply grateful, deeply indebted to the innocent world of plants which so redeems the guilty world of man. Among medieval mystics and alchemists the realization of this fact was very much alive, too.

Another sphere to which one can point in this matter of the senses is that of the whole method of *procreation* of the human race, which one feels instinctively is nearer the level of the animal world than innate human dignity demands and desires.

And finally one would point to the whole sphere of *metabolism*, particularly that of digestion, where a fine spiritual instinct might feel that the extensive destruction which works there (and it is possible to go into a detailed study of those processes and the poisonous nature of human excretion, etc.)—that this gives a picture of an almost tangible egotism. That the human excretions, the secretions, are charged with a kind of destructive egotism is again evidence of some kind of sickness, some kind of "fall". Indeed, in some agricultural experiments one can trace a sphere of destruction in us on which we naturally must live.

As a step, therefore, towards understanding that body which Christ has turned into a resurrection body, we should mobilize what we have left in us as spiritual instincts and see that natural, healthy man as he is and must be today still shows traces of a descent from what one could surmise as his original, better, more spiritual nature. We can perceive that there has been a descent; that it is one of the basic facts of human nature that we live as individuals of a species, as members of a universal earthly family, which are below what they might be and were at one time.

I have purposely put this in a somewhat simple way at first so that if we now go on to describe this disease in spiritual scientific terms we shall perhaps have brought a little of our heart into the matter. Because the worst error we could make is to describe these things, however brilliantly and cleverly, as a kind of theory and not be able to unite our sense of responsibility, the full forces of the artist, the heart-man in us, with this tremendous problem.

But now let us review the more specific description which Rudolf Steiner gives of the corruption of the human being. Perhaps the most extensive contribution towards this is to be found in the third and fourth lectures of the cycle "The World of the Senses and the World of the Spirit" given in Hanover in 1911. Steiner approaches the subject by viewing the disturbed interaction of the four bodies, of the four constituent members of the human being, which came about through that moral event which, in its mythological vesture, is called "The Fall From Paradise". He follows it, step by step, through the relationship, always, of two of the several bodies together. He begins by showing the disturbed balance between the physical and the etheric bodies, saying it resulted from the poison injected into the soul at that time; that in certain regions of the organism the physical body became more active, intruding upon the etheric body more than it should. Consequently certain organs are heavier and more material than they should be. Those are the sense organs.

Steiner then speaks in greater detail of the problem I first mentioned in biblical terms: "Their eyes were opened". He says that in the sphere of the sense organs the physical body asserts itself in an illegitimate way against the organizing forces of life in the etheric body. It is for this reason that our eyes are so comparatively material. An eye is less permeated by life than almost any part of the body; it is almost a telescopic lens, a photographic camera in its construction. If it had not been for the disturbance of The Fall we would not have this material eye as we have it now, but would have seeing activity in its place. That seeing activity would not observe the outer world of light and colour but would feel an immensely differentiated world of flowing, ruling will. Man would be aware that he lives in a universe which is essentially an ocean of spiritual will intensely differentiated. For our present perception the world appears in a great variety of created things. But the human body was originally so organized that man would not have seen the finished material creation but would have witnessed the process of creation, the will forces in action. Instead of the camera eye, we would have had a living activity which would have been able to touch, to sense in the most differentiated way, this great ocean of creative will. This would have been our seeing. In a similar way our hearing would have operated. Steiner says you can compare the set of little bones inside the ear with the keyboard of the piano—a surprising comparison; but he goes on to say it is something almost as material as a piano in its action. The physical forces assert themselves; they intrude into a sphere which should be fully permeated by the process of life. So we hear sounds externally, and as we know, very often suffer from them; whereas we should have had an organ of perception for the universal spiritual harmonies which permeate this ocean of differentiated, creative will.

Rudolf Steiner says that the only sense organ in which to some extent we can still feel the creative will is the hand. We can still use the hand freely as a kind of creative organ. We can also use it as a kind of sense organ, primarily for the sense of touch. The hand is in a halfway position between Paradise and The Fall. While our hands can still operate creatively, our eyes can not: our tongues hardly at all. With smell we come upon a kind of borderline. We know that we can smell in sleep, that a person's dreams can be influenced by scent. Experiments show that dreams can be induced to reproduce the scene of one's first conscious encounter with a particular smell. I am speaking only of the five senses, not attempting in this lecture to go into the full physiology of the twelve senses which Steiner differentiates. It is enough for the moment to see the principle by which he describes the disturbance of the interaction between the physical and etheric bodies.

Similarly he continues to describe the very complicated disharmony between the etheric and astral bodies. Where the etheric asserts its dominance over the astral, it involves the whole glandular system. As a result we can cry. Weeping is actually a result of The Fall. The glands react through over-assertion of the etheric forces on the astral. The secretion of tears is a result of the lack of balance. Perspiration is another one. "In the sweat of thy brow thou shalt eat thy bread" relates to the story of The Fall. Steiner specifically mentions perspiration, but generally he refers to the whole glandular system; the ductless glands, the whole endocrine system and their secretions, and ultimately the glands of the procreative organs operate as they do as a result of the disturbed balance brought about by the intrusion of the etheric upon the astral. And that too, as we shall see, has certain results on the whole material nature of man. It produces in him an almost animalistic enjoyment of sensuous comfort.

He then continues to show in another functional sphere, the digestive, that the astral overpowers the etheric, which is the reason why metabolism, digestion, is so destructive. If it were not so, if there were proper balance, our digestive system would operate as a creator of beauty, an etheric sculptor, so to say. It cannot do so. The intrusions of astrality over the etheric in the digestive sphere break down and destroy the food and produce those tremendous poisons which can be analysed in the secretions and excretions which result from metabolism.

Finally he describes the disturbed balance between man's ego and his astrality—and here I should like to translate from the German, as I go, in order to present the subject as nearly as possible in Rudolf Steiner's own words. Again he asks the question, "Just what was this temptation in Paradise?" Then, "Let us put it as simply as possible. It consisted in this, that Lucifer approached the human ego which man should have received in purity along with his astral body given him on the Moon, and said, 'Look here, Man, It's very boring always to walk about with this simple centre I AM and look at the rest of the world from outside. It would be much more interesting to plunge into the astral body. I will give you the power to do so, then you need not hold back but look into this astral double of yours. You can really immerse yourself in it. Of course you might get drowned in it, but I will help you. I will give you power so that you can immerse yourself without drowning.' So, the ego immersed itself—and became inoculated with Luciferic power. Thereby was brought about the preponderance of the power of the ego over the astral body."

As a result of this overpowering element in the ego, which is Luciferic, man is deeply bound into the processes of thought, feeling, and willing, which otherwise he would merely have used as instruments, somewhat as one plays upon musical instruments. But now he is drawn right into them. He lives in them, they absorb him. And because he retains his egotism by Luciferic means he makes thinking, feeling, and willing also Luciferic. That is the secret of the disturbed interaction between our ego and our astrality.

In this lecture Rudolf Steiner points to the first beginnings of man's spiritual training, the way by which he can escape his servitude. It reminds me of C. S. Lewis's description of the human ego as "a coward, a bully, a tale-bearer, and a liar", which is a remarkable description. You find in Steiner's lecture a similar description, but he indicates also the remedy. He gives four exercises: the training in wonder, in devotion to truth, in recognizing the marvellous spiritual ordering of the universe, and in man's voluntary cooperation with this order and integration into it. These are four ways in which the healing of the ego can be attempted. This healing may be begun now. Man may start within himself to reverse that process he once submitted to.

But before we discuss this reversal, and the activity we observe in Christ during his incarnation in Jesus up to the moment of His death, we must try to understand another riddle. How did it come about that our bodies altogether have become as material as they are? Steiner gives a fairly detailed description in Lecture Three of the cycle I mentioned and have quoted from. Most of what I shall now quote you will find in Lecture Four.

There he speaks in a broad way about the origin of matter. It is there that you find this great basic description: MATTER IS SPIRIT BURST INTO VISIBILITY. He makes the remarkable comparison to water falling and splashing in every direction as it meets a resisting surface. But, he says, imagine this to be the invisible spirit radiating. The spirit needs no obstruction, however, but can radiate by its own action, and in this radiation matter originates. Spirit bursts into visible matter. Matter everywhere can be called "broken spirituality". Paradisal man would have been fully permeated with spirit and so would have had no desire to burst into matter. He acquired a material body because the spirit permeating him was arrested by the disturbed harmonies in his organism. Thus, for the first time it became possible for him to have a corpse.

Then Steiner goes on to say that where the spirit struck against the physical body, allowing the etheric body to be overpowered, nerve substance came into being. If you study the whole cerebro-spinal system with the eye of the spiritual scientist you will find it the type of matter which has come about through the fact that spirit is arrested in a sphere where physical force can overpower the etheric in a disharmonious way. That is the basis for the creation of nerve matter. At the next stage, where the etheric overpowers the astral, muscular matter originates. Where the astral overpowers the etheric, there, in a somewhat complicated way, the substance of our bones comes into existence. But what was Paradisal Man like before all this happened? He was a form created by the Spirits of Form, created as an Imagination. This does not mean merely making a picture of what should be a living reality on the spiritual plane. In this context an *Imagination* is a spiritual entity, that lives, that is, that has being. That is the form of Paradisal Man. He was then permeated by the *Inspiration* of the Spirits of Movement which filled that imagination with motion; and he was further permeated by the Spirits of Wisdom, by their *Intuitions*. Finally he was given an aura by the Spirits of Will, the Thrones.

Such was Man before the Fall. Today, as a result of the broken harmony and the resulting fall into matter, we have in the bony system the frozen Imaginations of the Spirits of Form; in the muscular system the frozen Inspirations of the Spirits of Movement; and in the nervous system the frozen Intuitions of the Spirits of Wisdom. So we come to the level of existence, material existence, on which we now live. This is the complicated, the tragic history of the human being as we know him, as we know ourselves, as we live.

We must have all this tremendous and complex background in order to appreciate adequately the full significance of the redemptive act of Christ. We can see now, today, how essential the cosmic conceptions are for understanding the Christian Mysteries. With these facts one may attempt to understand the significance of the Incarnation and the redemptive action of Christ. It is not enough to leave it in the sphere of soul experience. We have to bring it into the sphere of the fullness of human nature, into that tangible sphere where we touch the body.

We can describe the Incarnation of Christ into the body of Jesus as a progressive activity, counteracting in that one body all the tragic history of the human race through the vast expanse of evolution. Let us briefly review those stages, which we can also trace in the biblical documents. We know that the Being of Christ entered into the human vehicle of Jesus at the Baptism in Jordan. For the first time in the history of mankind since the Fall a human being was possessed of an ego which was not human but macrocosmic. There followed the progressive permeation by Christ of the astral, etheric and physical bodies of Jesus.

The permeation of the astral body occurred in the Temptation which followed the Baptism immediately. Once again the Luciferic possibilities were laid before Him, but He refused to yield. He conquered the sick relationship between ego and astrality. On the basis of the biblical records one could almost show how at the end of the Temptation He had re-established the true human balance between angel and animal. You can read between the lines this fact of the re-established paradisal balance between ego and astrality.

From the Temptation we go to the next great landmark when the spirit of Christ permeates the etheric body of Jesus in what is described as the Transfiguration, a visionary manifestation of the fully transformed etheric body, which radiates light. No longer does it absorb the light of the Sun, it becomes itself a Sun. The biblical details are very illuminating. Through this event the proper relationship between the astral and ether bodies is re-established. Hereafter, even Christ's relationship to nature changes.

Finally in that sublime event of death the Being of Christ fully permeates the disturbed relationship between the etheric and physical bodies. Rudolf Steiner speaks of certain details here before that inner permeation was actually completed in death; when the processes of decomposition and combustion were finished and all that was left were the salt processes. These, within the body and in connection with the spices, dissolved so quickly that, during those three days when He was in the grave, dematerialization could take place not as a miracle but as the result of the three years of gradual, progressive re-establishment of the paradisal balance between the four constituent members of the human body. Christ came into the world as a pure spiritual ego, and by this ego counteracted death. Throughout three years he overcame the Luciferic sickness which had disturbed the original human harmony. As a result of this progressive permeation by the ego, conditions were created allowing dematerialization to take place; an un-doing, we might say, of the bursting of spirit into matter.

And now, one further word about the resurrection body itself, that body which appeared as related in the stories of the risen Christ and which seemed to possess the power of materializing and dematerializing at will. We find in these lectures of Rudolf Steiner which I have mentioned two sentences which are often overlooked. They are absolutely vital, because, after having described the various forms of matter and how each came about, he speaks of a kind of border-line matter, a peculiar substance which seems to exist on the border of the etheric and the physical. He says, "There is something which goes beyond ordinary matter, which is supersensible, and which we touch upon when we speak of the etheric body which *is* supersensible; something like a subtle, fine emanation of the etheric." These emanations, he says, "finer than the substance of nerves", this border-line sphere where the etheric enters into the physical, is something puzzling, tantalizing, even from the ordinary scientific point of view. I believe we have reason to suggest that this border-line matter becomes, in Christ's hands, the key to His materializations and de-materializations. In other words, it is the reconstituted paradisal organism of man.

But in all spiritual history, there is never a simple going back to what once was, to a reconstruction of that which was lost. That is against the spirit of true evolution. If something is recovered, it is recovered on a higher plane. The Bible does not lead back to Paradise, but forward to the New Jerusalem; that is to say, from the garden to the city, from the lesser to the greater. This reveals the great dynamic of spiritual evolution. Therefore, the body which Christ reconstructed is no longer merely the Imagination of the Spirits of Form, the Inspiration of the Spirits of Movement, the Intuition of the Spirits of Wisdom. It has become something more, something He can handle, materialize, and de-materialize at will.

That, I believe, is the closest description—spiritual scientific description—of the resurrection body of

Christ which we can today give. In another cycle, "From Jesus to Christ", Steiner used a special phrase for that particular reality of the resurrection body. He calls it the Phantom of Man. He makes it quite clear that the Phantom is not an etheric body but the reconditioned spiritual essence of the physical body. The Risen Christ can materialize and de-materalize this "Phantom" at will. In that cycle Steiner also points out in detail how in the early days of Christianity these things were still known and discussed, albeit they were very soon lost. We may gather that both the Evangelist John and the Apostle Paul had this knowledge. In the first Epistle to the Corinthians Paul proclaims that the human race would be able to partake of this reconditioned paradisal body. St. Paul's phrase is "The Second Adam" who is "a quickening spirit"—a beautiful expression. "As in the first Adam all died so in the Second Adam all shall be made alive." This is really the secret of the original Christian wisdom of the resurrection of the body, and its significance for the human race.

But it should be remembered that no one, not even in the most primitive Christian creeds, ever spoke of the resurrection of "the bodies" but always of "the body"—the whole body of humanity—a type of creation Steiner calls the Group-soul type. The resurrection applies to us who are now living, and to those who will come after us, and to ourselves as we come again. We continue to touch hands with each other. As Rudolf Steiner puts it, we can think of the Phantom as a cell that will multiply, at first imperfectly. He says that the expression "put on the resurrection body" as used by Paul is a quaint but accurate description, a true picture of what can happen to us.

We should not attempt to discuss these matters merely as a subject of interest, but we should feel responsibility towards them. What we have tried to do, with all its limitations and imperfections, is to give an impulse towards our entering into the renewal of the resurrection body. This can be done outside the Anthroposophical Society, through various forms of Christian organization, but, so far as we know, there is no other movement in the world where these things are so deeply understood; where they are so permeated with thought, reason, and understanding. And this is the unique contribution which our Society has to make.

THE VISION OF CHRIST IN THE ETHERIC WORLD

A week ago we attempted something very daring, and you may remember that we travelled a fairly long distance in our effort to understand what we describe as the Resurrection Body of Christ: also, that we aimed not only at a theoretical yet reverent study of this Being but led up to the conviction that it has something to do with us, with the whole evolution of humanity. What was described as the Resurrection Body of Christ can gradually, in a process extending over the rest of evolution, be absorbed by at least that part of the human species which does its share in the process. Strictly speaking this is really what the term *Chymical Marriage* suggests.

You remember that Rudolf Steiner occasionally refers to that Mystical Marriage which some of the earlier mystics mentioned; that kind of union which opened the soul to the spiritual world. But in certain circumstances he uses the term *Chymical Marriage* precisely for this gradual absorption of the resurrection forces of Christ into the human organism, by which that harmony is gradually re-established which through the Fall was lost. We saw how this loss of harmony between the physical and etheric bodies affected the senses; between the etheric and astral bodies affected the glandular system; between the astral and etheric reversed, affected the digestive system; and finally how the disharmony between the ego and soul forces affected thought, feeling, and willing. We saw how all can gradually be balanced so that in the fullness of time humanity can reach the stage where death as we know it ceases to be. Then, the ability to use the power of materialization and de-materialization at will can be shared by that part of humanity which has been truly developed. This part will then pass on from the Earth to Jupiter.

But now tonight we are trying to tackle an entirely different aspect of the problem. Perhaps it is important to realize first that if we speak of that renewed Presence of Christ in the etheric world of which Rudolf Steiner speaks, we are dealing with something quite different from what we considered last week. I will take my start from one sentence in the lecture published in English under the title "The Event of the Appearance of Christ in the Etheric World", given in Carlsruhe on January 25th, 1910. The sentence reads: "The greatest mystery of our time is this one concerning the second coming of Christ." January 25th, 1910, however, was not the first time he mentioned this fact. It is interesting to know that he first spoke of the Etheric Christ in our time in Stockholm in December, 1909. Unfortunately there are no notes of this lecture, but there is an interesting anecdote connected with it. It was in the time of Steiner's connection with the old Theosophical Society. The group leader in Stockholm, in addition to his Theosophical interests, had a special interest in astrology and cast a horoscope for the date on which Steiner was expected to give an important members' lecture there. To his great horror he found that the constellation was truly awful, so he approached Rudolf Steiner about a week before, warned him about it, in fact did his best to persuade him to postpone this lecture, saying he could not possibly give it under such an awful constellation. Needless to say, Steiner took no notice of that fact, and it is perhaps worth remembering that the actual first statement to members about this great mystery—the greatest of the twentieth century—was made on a day which, according to traditional astrological calculations, was really a black day if ever there was one. You can hardly have a better example of Rudolf Steiner's tremendously positive attitude, his great faith in these matters.

After speaking on this subject a month or so later for the first time in Germany, he gave that cycle of lectures now published under the title "The Christ Impulse and the Development of Ego Consciousness" and then on March 6th the first lecture in Stuttgart on "The Re-appearance of Christ in the Etheric". In the following years he continued to refer to this event time and time again. Right away, in the first lecture of the cycle given in Carlsruhe, he speaks of those first important years of this century during which he anticipated that the first experiences of the Christ would take place. He says: "The first indications of these new soul faculties will begin to appear relatively soon now among isolated individuals. They will become more apparent in the middle of the fourth decade of the century, somewhere between 1930 and 1940. The years 1933, 1935, and 1937 will be especially significant. Faculties which are quite unusual for human beings will then manifest themselves as wholly natural abilities."

Now these dates have a remarkable connection with

the early dates of the founding of Christianity. In a members' meeting it may be permissible to pass on a contribution towards understanding this tremendous mystery: it was made by one of our English friends. You may remember that in a lecture given by Dr. Steiner on September 2nd, 1923 in London, following the courses in Ilkley and Penmaenmawr, he speaks of the various planetary spheres and their relationships to human life on earth. He speaks of the Moon as the residuum of the forces of procreation, and of the Saturn sphere as that in which the great cosmic memory rests, where in particular all the great moral deeds of human history are, so to say, received and recorded; in due course their karmic consequences enter into the evolution of humanity. Not just there, but also in other contexts, Rudolf Steiner often refers to the rhythm in which this cosmic memory works and which is indicated to earthly observation in the actual time the planet Saturn requires to go around the Sun once, which is not quite thirty years. The English friend noted the time required for the first appearance of Christ; its preparation through the birth of the two children and the building up of the earthly vehicle of the Jesus individuality—that masterpiece of creation—which then became the body of Christ; the whole extending over approximately thirty-three years. Looking at that one Christmas lecture where Steiner speaks of these rhythms, our English friend suggested that you think of this first period of Christ's appearance on earth as being received into the Saturn Sphere; multiply the period of His life by the Saturn period around the Sun and you get the time when that great earthly event reached the utmost circumference of the planetary sphere of Saturn, the utmost depths of cosmic consciousness, and then began to travel back to earth. With more detailed calculation, taking the Mystery of Golgotha as the starting point (which Dr. Steiner fixed as April 3rd, A.D.33), you come to the year 1935 as the year when that double rhythm is completed.

I remember vividly the picture our friend gave, saying, "Think of a pond, a quiet bit of water, and a stone thrown into its centre; then the ripples travel out until they reached the shore when they are thrown back again to the centre. The Incarnation of Christ is like a stone thrown into the ocean of humanity. The effects of it spread from the earth into the cosmos in the Saturn rhythm until they reached the furthest point in the Saturn sphere, travelled back, and began striking on to the shore of human history in 1935."

But be this as it may, we have Steiner's indication which I quote again: "Faculties which are quite unusual for human beings will then manifest themselves as wholly natural abilities." And further: "At this time great changes will take place and biblical prophecies will be fulfilled. Everything will be transformed for the souls who are sojourning on earth and also for those who are no longer within a physical body. Regardless of where they are, they are approaching entirely new faculties. Everything is changing; but the most significant event is a decisive transformation of the soul faculties of man."

Now those times have passed, and we may well wonder whether they have had a measure of fulfilment.

Even if we doubt a little, it seems to me this is perhaps partly owing to the fact that we have never quite fully understood what Steiner meant by saying that biblical prophecies will be fulfilled. I think even in our own circles there is often a great deal of—almost prejudice, shall I say, about this; because certain biblical passages dealing obviously with the so-called Second Coming are themselves misunderstood. A misinterpreted biblical prophecy often hangs like a cloud before our free understanding of these events. I will therefore cite a few passages and try to interpret them in the way I think they should be interpreted. Then, instead of clouding, they should illuminate our view.

To begin we must say that there is no such expression in the whole Bible, in the New Testament at any rate, as "Second Coming". It just does not exist. It has gradually crept into the popular use of religious language, but otherwise does not exist. There is one term in the so-called apocalyptic passages of the New Testament which can, among other things, mean "coming". But nowhere do you find the adjective "second". Because this matter is so important I will write the Greek word on the blackboard. Written in our alphabet and pronounced in ordinary English, it is *parousia*. Now we have to consider something important in translating from an ancient language to a modern, or for that matter from an Eastern to a Western. Modern, Western languages are analytical; they are split up. The comprehensive meaning of words which we find in ancient languages, or in Eastern languages today, presents a problem; in Russian even more so. When we look up this word in a dictionary we find four different meanings. What generally happens in such a case is that one picks out the meaning one thinks most suitable; but then obviously something arbitrary comes in. A choice and a judgment made from a particular point of view play a large part in interpreting the meaning. That is what happens in translating this keyword into the English Bible.

Its first meaning is *presence* and that is the original meaning. Then comes the second which may mean *advent* or *coming*. Thirdly it means *indwelling*, and then also *aid* or *help*. In the original text of the New Testament this word is used for those prophecies which speak of a future, new Presence of Christ in human evolution. Nothing less than the comprehensive fullness of the four-fold meaning is adequate for translating those passages. You can almost take the four meanings as the points of a meditation. You know Rudolf Steiner sometimes gave meditations in that way, giving just points and leaving it to his pupils to work them out into meditative lines. If we did so in this case we would find that there is implied in his concept of the Presence of Christ the fundamental idea that His Being is an abiding Presence in human evolution. Then our meditative progress from the *presence* to *coming* or *advent* might be made in the following way. We have learned from Rudolf Steiner not only to think of, but really to understand, the Being of Christ as a Living Presence. We know that one of the basic manifestations of every living being is rhythm; life essentially manifests itself in rhythmical form: in expansion and contraction, in ebb and flow, in coming and going.

This is the fundamental concept in Anthroposophy regarding the Presence of Christ in humanity: there is not a static Presence, having the same place and the same pressure all the time, but a coming and going, an ebb and flow. You may recall those relevant two lines of the Christmas Foundation Meditation which refer to Christ: "In den Weltenrhythmen Seelenbegnadend". (In world-wide rhythms bestowing grace on human souls.) There, in one of the fundamental things Rudolf Steiner gave at what may have been the biggest landmark in the history of the Anthroposophical Movement, you have that concept of the Christ bestowing grace on human souls through cosmic rhythms. There are times when He presses upon human souls, others when He withdraws; as does the great ebb and flow of the cosmic ocean of the spiritual world in which He lives and moves and has His rhythmical being.

This so-called Second Coming, then, simply suggests that we are now reaching a period of history when in a different, transformed way a renewed Presence, a renewed full pressure is to be expected. And we may bear in mind that Steiner suggests that under certain circumstances there will be an astral coming; and finally a coming of Christ in the ego. These suggestions give more light, more content to this fundamental concept of the rhythmical Presence of Christ in human evolution. Then, in connection with this *parousia* of which the New Testament speaks, we add a further concept which you find, developed of course, in Rudolf Steiner's writings: that this new Coming is not one visible in the flesh but which can be described as an indwelling in that inward sphere of the etheric into which we may penetrate. He does indeed come in order to help humanity.

This leads us on immediately to the second biblical prophecy which requires elucidation. If we read these biblical passages in the language we normally use, we very much doubt whether this Coming, this renewed coming of Christ, is a help. In fact, in traditional teachings Christ usually appears as a judge. He comes "to judge the quick and the dead", and so on. In other words, popular opinion connects that renewed Presence of Christ with what is generally referred to as the Last Judgment, or the Eternal Judgment. And here we perhaps come up against the bias of the reformers who have translated the Greek Bible into English. They simply have the prevalent idea of the early seventeenth century about Christ as the Judge, a kind of early Puritanism affecting the translation from Greek. I often quote a striking phrase of H. D. Morton in "The Steps of The Master". He says, "The Bible you have is written in the heavily embroidered draperies of Jacobean English; very beautiful, completely out of date, and tremendously misleading." This is an adequate description, and no passages are more misleading than those dealing with the renewed Coming of Christ. In this translation, you can almost disregard the Book of Revelation, and also the apocalyptic chapters in the Gospels.

When we consider the phrase "Last Judgement" we need not give the Greek word for it as we have adopted that in modern English. We know it very well, this word for judgment. It is—"Crisis"—which is just the old Greek word spelled in English letters. You need only put that word into the context of the New Testament and you get at once a different feeling; that *parousia* will produce a *crisis*. Of course you may say a crisis is a judgment. The economic crisis of 1929 which this country remembers so well was without doubt a judgment on the prevailing economic system. In that sense, international crises are judgments upon our international dealings. Yet this is an entirely different concept of a judgment; not a legalistic one, of a being sitting up in judgment and passing sentence on others, but a judgment inherent in the progress of human destiny. That is the significance of the Coming of the Etheric Christ being the cause of a crisis.

Now the Greek word for eternal is *aeon*; again a word which has been taken into modern English. It is a kind of poetic expression borrowed from Ancient Greek to denote a period of history; in fact, a period of history defined by a cosmic background. That is the old concept of an *aeon*—a period in human development which is fundamentally part of a cosmic rhythm. This is suggested in the biblical prophecies to which Steiner refers; because of the Etheric Presence of Christ a *crisis of the age*, an historic crisis, will be brought about.

It is hardly necessary to remind ourselves that we live in critical days, but we will not dwell on this. We may recall that Rudolf Steiner speaks in quite specific terms about this age. He gives us the picture of the sequence of post-Atlantean history, proceeding in seven great epochs, the present being the fifth epoch. The beginning of it is marked by an astronomical event, the movement of the vernal point of the Sun, where it rises in the spring equinox, from Aries (the Ram) into Pisces (Fishes). This took place in the year 1413. But this fifth epoch is not just another one like the preceding, as five follows four. It means a fundamental turning-point of earth evolution as far as human consciousness is concerned. Steiner describes how right to the end of the fourth epoch, although it contained the Mystery of Golgotha, human consciousness still lived in a kind of dreamy, cosmic, inherited instinct; that in a sense the last remnants of what we generally describe as clairvoyance survived, legitimately, if only in rudimentary form. Only with the beginning of the fifth epoch have we entered fully into earthly circumstances. From then on it had to be that all the cosmic legacy is spent, and for a time we are as poor as can be, spiritually. Therefore this age, this fifth epoch, is the crucial one.

It has struck me that it may not be accidental that not long after that cosmic moment this continent was discovered, or opened up, and gradually the foundations were laid for the American Nation. Somehow this seems to me an historic creation more symbolic of the fifth post-Atlantean epoch than anything else. The European continent has to catch up now. If you go to Germany you see how it catches up; how to some extent what was the beautiful, visible embodiment of some of the ancient legacies—the cathedrals, the works of art, the whole surviving culture which was still inspired by the sunset of cosmic spirituality—is now all in ruins. There, what thrived in the beginning of the fourth epoch has been brought to a finish. Here in America, the fifth epoch started right away from scratch, so to speak. It was built up by the displaced people from Europe; the throw-offs, even some criminal elements. But all were pioneers in building the new American Nation, significantly at the beginning of this fifth epoch. The more I move about on this continent the more I feel that it has some strange relationship, some beautiful, promising, challenging relationship to the very character of this epoch. These succeeding crises in which we find ourselves are not only immediate problems of our own making. They have come upon us because we live in this vital turning-point of earth evolution. And how fast are we moving towards the end of the century when Rudolf Steiner said the final fate of the planet Earth will be decided! It is not the Last Judgment, but that evolutionary crisis which the Advent of the Etheric Christ will bring.

And now one last remark in connection with these elementary facts. In the New Testament there occurs that phrase "The Last Day", and here the translation is adequate. I often remind people in this connection of a European custom referring, in business jargon, to the Last Day, or "the ultimo": the day the accounts have to be made up, you have to prepare your balance, send in your income tax return, and all that sort of thing—the end of the financial year. That is the concept of "The Last Day" in the New Testament, which is to say business does not stop after the book-balancing. There may be Last Days in human history whose characteristics are that accounts have to be made up, debts paid, balance sheets issued, income tax paid—all those things which in some measure we have begun to experience in this century. We are paying debts, cultural debts, either voluntarily or under compulsion, on a big scale. We are moving rapidly towards such a Last Day. But the great thing is that human history goes on afterwards. We may see the coming of the Etheric Christ as, if I may put it so, the opening up of new credit to humanity, but only on condition that a balance sheet has been made, debts paid, and the past wound up. So we come to realize how true is Rudolf Steiner's sentence: "biblical prophecies will be fulfilled." And he goes on: "Everything will be changed for the souls who are sojourning on earth, and also for those who are no longer in the physical body." It is then that he speaks of the new faculties developing.

Now let me start again from another biblical expression, moving from the Gospels into the Epistles of St. Paul. Paul is the first one who ever spoke of the Etheric Christ, in what is generally regarded by historians as the oldest part of the New Testament; that is, the two Epistles to the Thessalonians. They speak not of Jesus, not even of Christ; they speak primarily of the Etheric Coming of Christ. In those passages he elaborates to some extent a phrase which occurs also in the Gospels, that He will come "in the clouds". Now there is a key word to that whole sphere, the Greek word *nephele* from which nebulous is derived, and Nifelheim, and such like. One wonders just what this means. As I have sometimes spoken to public audiences on this subject I will tell you how I introduce it because I think it may interest you to see how you can speak today, quite openly, about these things.

I say—(and this is taken from Rudolf Steiner's "How To Attain Knowledge of the Higher Worlds")—take a grain of wheat, a living one, and put it on your left hand; then put a perfect imitation of it—in plaster of paris, or plastic of any kind—on your right hand. Show them to people in an ordinary city audience and, if the imitation is perfect, they will not notice the difference. If you give the imitation to a farmer he is bound to sense it. You need not go far back in history to find that people generally would have seen the difference, because the last remnants of clairvoyance were still operating and could see the aura of a living grain. The Greek word for cloud, *nephele*, does include that concept of the great realm of the clouds which permeates, but also surrounds in a subtle way, all living things. In Anthroposophical terms we would say it was the etheric aura of organic matter, of living things. That is part of the cloud.

But that is not all. Here we proceed to certain considerations which I think belong essentially to our attempt to remove some of the blinds our souls now have against the vision of the Etheric Christ. We have plenty of material from Anthroposophy for doing so; learning better to understand the visible clouds in the sky, which at least reflect—but you will see it is more than that—that part of the sphere in which the Etheric Presence will be observed. As you may know, ordinary clouds are a great scientific mystery. They are colder and heavier than the surrounding air, and yet they float. There are plenty of theories for this, but none very satisfactory. Recently I flew one day from Louisville to Chicago, and on the plane we were given a little booklet as an introduction to the meteorological phenomena which we could see. There it was stated that "the clouds are suspended by an uprush of cold air". But as everybody knows, cold air does not rush up. It may do so in front of a mountain, but there is nothing flatter than the country between Louisville and Chicago. There is nothing to induce an uprush of cold air. How, then, are those clouds suspended? It is by the action of the etheric forces. This also explains that other great mystery in nature, the rise of the sap in spring. Scientific theory says it is due to capillary action, osmosis, etcetera. But you can answer, then why does that action work in the spring and not in the fall? Physical laws operate all the year round; water boils at 100° centigrade both in spring and fall. There is no seasonal exception to physical law. But this rising of the sap is due to the anti-gravitational forces of the etheric world, of which the sun is the great centre. Those forces modern science has completely failed to understand. In a famous quotation from Ruskin is a beautiful summing-up of the difficulty. He spoke of Newton—who could easily explain how the apple fell from the tree on his head, creating the legend of how he came to study the law of gravitation. But Ruskin said: "Newton has never explained how the apple got up there"—which is the problem in a nutshell—the question of the reality and the nature of the etheric forces.

For the Anthroposophist the etheric forces are not complicated chemical or physical forces but have their own character. The Greeks were far in advance of modern science in these matters. They had three words for "life": *zoe*, the life of the spirit; *psyche*, the life of the soul; and *bios* (from which biology is derived), denoting organic life, the life of the etheric world. To use a strange phrase of Rudolf Steiner's, "the etheric world is essentially negative space". It has spatial qualities. If we take gravitational space as positive—that with which we normally operate—we would have to ascribe, not in moral terms but in mathematical terms, the quality of "negative" to etheric space. It works in an opposite direction.

The visible clouds *are* suspended by etheric activity. And I can tell you a little detail from Rudolf Steiner which throws still more light on the subject. It is a fact that near Stuttgart you sometimes see in the spring that the clouds assume most peculiar shapes. They look like primeval monsters; like dragons really. We asked Rudolf Steiner whether that had any significance, and he said, "Yes! Remember that around here, a little to the east of the city, there is the greatest deposit of fossils in Central Europe; fossils of primeval animals, of the saurian type. And the forces which in the old days worked on those animals, giving shape to the dragons and saurians, operate up above in their kind of cosmic laboratory. They use the clouds as their plastic material. There you can still study the etheric formative forces which were special in this part of the world." And you may remember how in certain lectures he speaks even of the glow of the sky as a visible reflection of the etheric. He says that we see blue because we see the air illumined by light against a dark background; that cosmic darkness is really the ether.

So the etheric world is not as hidden as we often think it is when we begin to read about it and study it.

There are certain aspects of the etheric world which touch even our senses. Steiner said once that Stifter's grandmother—(Stifter was an Austrian writer he was very fond of)—was far wiser than the most modern meteorologist, because she said that the clouds are the washing of the Mother of God, hung up in the sky by the angels. This is a kind of primitive, imaginative expression of the fact that clouds are not only material; they are the visible manifestation of the astral sphere. Therefore, all those references in biblical passages to the clouds are simply—well, speaking in a different language. But they speak essentially of the etheric sphere mentioned by Steiner as that in which the new Presence of Christ can be found. He then goes on to speak of changing faculties, both here and in the life after death; and in those very chapters in Thessalonians you find a reference to this, again camouflaged in the old translations. St. Paul says, "We shall be lifted up—caught up to meet the Lord in the air—and those alive shall have no advantage over those who sleep." That is the old way of putting it.

Remember that Rudolf Steiner speaks in those lectures about a movement of humanity into that sphere of the clouds. Actually, the manifestation, the advent of Christ in the etheric world is a meeting; the Christ, in his rhythmical Presence, presses forward into the etheric sphere, into the sphere of life, but humanity—and it is vital that Steiner says "on its natural path of development"—touches on that sphere in its soul region. It is the first glimmering of an awakening of new senses *which can see the etheric.* One might think it is a first awakening of our etheric eyes. "You see, we think we see with our eyes," he says; "but we don't literally see with the eyes we have in here"—and he pointed to his eyes. "They are a kind of microscope, or telescope, or camera, a fairly dead body in us. We see by means of it, with etheric activity."

He explains the physiologically perceived colours as the result of etheric activity. If you look at green and afterwards at a white sheet of paper you see red (literally, not in anger!). This seeing red is due to the continuation of the etheric activity of the eye, which answers to the impressions of colours. We see a balance. We never see an actual colour as it is, but always a balance. We produce complementary colours through the etheric activity of our eye; and what we see, the final physical effect, is a balance. Balance is so deeply built into man that all our relationships are balanced, or ought to be. (If you are sick, of course, your balance is disturbed.)

I have often wondered—and I say this with some caution because it is more an idea of my own—whether that very intensification of the natural etheric activity, to which we owe even our ordinary sense perceptions, becomes more and more subtle, and more and more active. Some people, I realize, can experience that; for instance, the activity of the etheric eye before it enters fully into a physical instrument is one of the first things you can experience in the process of waking up. It is just here that the etheric body begins to awake, naturally, and it is the etheric forces which see. In his lectures "From Jesus to Christ", Steiner suggests that it is our own etheric activity which lightens up that sphere in which the Etheric Christ is present. In one sentence only he says this, but he does say it—that through our own activity we can shed some light. It is an activity which in its clarity, and beauty, can be strengthened through moral development; not necessarily only through the specific spiritual discipline of the meditative path, but really through moral development as a whole. That moral progress improves the etheric light we can shed from our own eyes, from our own heads, into the etheric world, to lighten up the Christ.

But Rudolf Steiner goes further than that, and makes perhaps the most puzzling, the strangest of his remarks: that there will be times as the century progresses when the etheric Christ assumes such a visible form that He can be seen with physical eyes. It will be only the initiate, he says, who can really see that it is an etheric body. He would feel that it was the Christ form who appeared in a room. But, Steiner said once, no one would ever see Him go down the stairs. There we come near to what we were speaking about a week ago, that ultimate consummation of the resurrection body. I quoted one sentence from the cycle "The World of the Senses and the World of the Spirit" which indicated that there is some kind of etheric materiality, what Steiner called "etheric matter". It seems that under certain circumstances it can be so condensed that it assumes the appearance of a physical presence, and the picture we try to describe would not be complete if we did not mention this. Rudolf Steiner went so far as to say that a figure like this might even appear in an assembly of people and throw an illuminating remark into the discussion. Then it would depart, and nobody would know that it was the Etheric Christ Who had spoken. Steiner spoke very definitely about this.

Now whether these things have happened, whether they are happening, whether they are becoming more frequent, is a great question. One meets people—particularly in Central Europe—who speak of experiences which sound authentic. Naturally one keeps an open mind for such things, and is very careful. But I should like to make one general observation. It seems to me very doubtful whether those first experiences which Steiner foreshadows and promises would take place among Anthroposophists. I am inclined to think the very opposite is the case. It may rather be with people on the fringe of the movement, somewhat connected with us, not those who are within it and are its responsible leaders. You might find—it is open to question, but I will put it before you—a hint of this in Steiner's first Mystery Play. Remember Theodora who has the vision. She moves in the circle of Benedictus but she obviously is not one of his disciples. She is a striking character right at the beginning of that play, the one who sees the Etheric Christ there. She is a visitor, a welcome visitor in the house of Maria, but she is not one of the intimate disciples of Benedictus. Not wishing to overstress the fact, I nevertheless think it suggests to us that we should never think that we as Anthroposophists have a monopoly of such experiences.

Rudolf Steiner suggests that it may be that this vital experience comes to somebody as it did to Paul in his experience at Damascus—a biblical scene to which he often refers. I think one must take that statement with some qualification because the Damascus experience as described in the Bible shows a certain violence. Paul is thrown from his horse, he cannot speak, he is blind for three days, goes without food, and so on. Steiner never suggests that the modern experience of the Etheric Christ is accompanied by any such violence. The main point of comparison, I think, is that Paul saw (*out of due time*, which may explain the violence)—he saw into the etheric sphere. The time had not come for humanity to do so. Possibly, however, there are other points of comparison. He was a seeker, but one who looked first entirely in the wrong direction. Then, even the setting in Damascus seems to be suggestive, since all Eastern geography is symbolic. Damascus is situated in the desert, inhabited even in those days by Arab tribes. We know what kind of associations the Arabic spirit calls up in those of us who have read and lived for some time with the last lectures which Rudolf Steiner gave in the summer of 1924; those karma lectures where Arabism has become almost a symbol not only for people who lived in the desert but who cultivated the desert of intellectualism. Within the desert is Damascus, one of the most beautiful oases in the world; a beautiful city with palms and natural springs like a symbol of the etheric region in the centre of a great, dry, sandy desert. And there comes the man who has persecuted the visible adherents of the historic Jesus. There, turning his back on Palestine, marching North, his eyes open and he sees, characteristically, not Christ—"Who art thou?"—"I am Jesus whom thou persecutest". In a sense it is the Christ incarnated not in the flesh but in the etheric body of Jesus.

If we have said that it is only our own light, our own moral qualities which may lighten up that sphere, let us remember that Steiner also says that the etheric body of Christ is in need of strengthening in substance; that the awe and wonder of our thought, the mercy and love of our hearts, the conscientiousness of our deeds, are material that strengthens His etheric body. Thus, we can do something about it ourselves. Although he stresses the fact that it is a natural event which takes place, he also suggests that this event comes today to a humanity which has grown beyond the childhood of early Christianity and is reaching manhood, showing its responsibility in cooperation, and which adds both to the light and to the substance of that experience. Even in this, dear friends, I feel we have no monopoly. That can be done outside our ranks. But, as I said last week, we do have a heavy responsibility in that we are the only people who will understand. And it will be vital that these events should find understanding. Our society is the cosmic organ of understanding for these events.

This is perhaps the thought with which I may conclude. For a moment we may reflect on the fact that today a society entrusted with such an enormous responsibility has no longer the shelter which such societies had in ancient times. Then the organs for cosmic understanding were confined to the sacred precincts of the mystery temples, and only those were allowed to share in their knowledge whom the priests and initiates selected, whom they recognized in their karmic background and in their aura as potential candidates for the mysteries. This is no longer the case.

Today the cosmic organ for understanding the mysteries in human history is a society open to everybody who cares to walk in and become a member. That is a tremendous change. Perhaps this will also help us to understand some of the tragic events which have moved in upon us in recent years, from which our movement has suffered and with which we are still battling.

The very fact that we are not a selected body, selected by the superior wisdom of an initiate, but that we have come together through our free choice, with all our imperfections, will explain the shortcomings of this cosmic organ of cognition we are supposed to be. At the same time we cannot forget that this is what we *are* supposed to be.

So let me conclude, as we did last time, with the suggestion that whatever we may be, to be a cosmic vehicle for understanding is our greatest responsibility. However these profound events may take place, anywhere, we have no right to judge. But we know that in our Society is the only place where they will be really understood. This is our responsibility.